UP LIBERTY STREET

poems by

Erica Bodwell

Finishing Line Press
Georgetown, Kentucky

UP LIBERTY STREET

Copyright © 2017 by Erica Bodwell
ISBN 978-1-63534-162-1 First Edition
All rights reserved under International and Pan-American Copyright Conventions.

No part of this book may be reproduced in any manner whatsoever without written permission from the publisher, except in the case of brief quotations embodied in critical articles and reviews.

ACKNOWLEDGMENTS

Alliterati—"Up Liberty Street,"
Cactus Heart—"And What Was It Like,"
Coal Hill Review—"Camp, 1979,"
Emerge Literary Journal—"1980s,"
Hot Metal Bridge—"The Girl In the Bed,"
The Orange Room Review—"Dragons,"
Persephone's Daughters—"Accident" and "Summertime"

Publisher: Leah Maines

Editor: Christen Kincaid

Cover Art: Elizabeth Becker

Author Photo: Aaron Baker, Mulberry Creek Photography

Cover Design: Elizabeth Maines

Printed in the USA on acid-free paper.
Order online: www.finishinglinepress.com
also available on amazon.com

Author inquiries and mail orders:
Finishing Line Press
P. O. Box 1626
Georgetown, Kentucky 40324
U. S. A.

Table of Contents

1980s 1

Up Liberty Street 2

Dragons 4

Ode to the Yellow Sparkle Snare Drum 5

Trenton, 1978 6

Summertime 7

Once, In the Middle of the Night 8

Camp, 1979 9

1980s 10

Accident 11

Natural History 12

Yellow House 13

The Winter Inside 15

Loops 16

And What Was It Like 17

Lucifer 18

The Girl in the Bed 19

1980s 20

Leap 21

Breezy Point, Queens 22

Were This the House 23

for Jane

1980s

I used to walk home past a cemetery and a boy who smoked
Out among the graves. One night he called me over in a voice so low

And throaty I thought it was a ghost. He smelled of gasoline,
Detergent. When the flame leapt from his lighter and unmasked

His Matt Dillon face, I let him yank
His hands through my hair and move my mouth where he wanted it.

I liked to grab his black bandanna and bind his hands, watch him work
His way free. Some nights, he'd stay bound.

Up Liberty Street

Summer 1982 split and peeling,
Days spent swigging Pepsi Lite,
Nights burnished and lotioned.
Dean Chiovoloni is teaching me to blow
Globes of spit off the end of my tongue
And the words to *You Shook Me All Night Long.*
His tongue slides out and a bubble floats off past the porch railing.
It's beyond easy, Dean says, Just do this.

She was a fast machine, she kept her motor clean.
She was the best damn woman that I've ever seen.
Simon sits on the stoop mastering his one-handed rolling technique.
His long fingers hold the joint like a diploma
He presents to his mouth.

He leans back on his elbows
And looks at me from under eyelashes
So long they curl up and touch his eyelids.
She had those sightless eyes, telling me no lies.
Knocking me out with those American thighs.
Dean is talking, talking, talking, feeding me lyrics,
Hopping from foot to foot. Dean,
The reason we all got front-hook bras,
Who taught the art of one-handed unsnapping,
Who taught us not to turn our backs.

Taking more than her share, she had me fighting for air,
She told me to come but I was already there.
Dean says, Do the rest yourself.
I land a wet orb at the hem of Simon's basketball shorts.
Dean says, Nice.

And the walls were shaking,
Earth was quaking,
My mind was aching
And we were making it.

Yooooou shook me alllll night long,
Yeah yooooooou shook me all night long.
I keep pulling up my tube top
And Simon tells me to stop fidgeting
And sit down between his legs.
Ashes fall into my hair. Dean says,
Sing it again.

Dragons

She hated them: my brothers. She hated that they drank a gallon of milk a day, that their voices cracked, that they lived beyond edge of the map, beyond her, the accustomed Mother.

She hated their babyhoods, their uncircumcised penises that peed straight up, the way one sucked his thumb and twisted his hair into tight knots, their open mouths like baby birds crying.

They were the price she paid to get another girl, to keep her numbers high, to put tiny plastic barrettes in our hair, to sigh to her friends, the girls are so easy.

Out of her reach, they punched each other on the way to the bathroom and got high in their bedrooms. Their smoldering friends came up the tree and through the window and

she'd put on a show for them, flirting, touching their downy teenage forearms, saying oh Kenny, oh Dean, and for those minutes she's at the Snowball Dance

and three of them move her around the waxy gym floor for the whole school to see.

Ode to the Yellow Sparkle Snare Drum

Power sparkler, noise maker,
Percussive silencer of sisters. I'll stand on tiptoes
To pound you, slam you, slap you, tighten
Your tension rods, snap your snare head.

I'll carry sticks hard and long
For you. You saved me

From the flute and its case like a doll's casket,
From tiny boxes of thin reeds that splinter like envy,

From white plastic chairs in the wind section.
Silver-circled dazzler, I'll snap my sticks into the clip

Screwed to your hoop, slide you into the plush red
Of your slick hard case, keep you

From dust and snakes. O yellow sparkle snare drum
Thank you for giving me a reason to walk with weapons.

Trenton, 1978

Once I was enrolled for an entire week
In my cousin Danny's fourth grade class, a scheme
My mother and aunt cooked up
In the kitchen hung with cheesecloth bags

Of dripping yogurt, *because you guys need to see
How people less fortunate than you live.*
Henry, with coppery brown legs and bright white socks,
Would stand behind me in line and whisper,

I like you and I would beg God in urgent silence,
Make him stop, and he would, and then I would command God,
Make him say it again and then he would.
My stepfather and uncle would argue, my uncle

Would slam his fist, *At least we tried!* The cousins
Had adopted a girl that summer. *They're only taking her
Because she's half-black.* She was so beautiful
With her crazy hair and burnished skin and emerald eyes.

I felt bad for the other cousins and their faces like paste.
I loved sitting with Danny between my knees, peeling strips
Of skin from his pale shoulders, pulling up my shorts
To show him my tan lines, my skin that never burned.

Summertime

n. 1. *Female.* As in sleepaway camp, as in sleeping away, as in away from _____, as in blue, as in moon, as in second full, as in July, as in lake's edge, as in silvery. 2. *Warm.* As in open windows, as in neighbors can hear, as in heatless VW van, as in who cares. 3. *Water.* As in swim, as in length of every pool, as in breath-holder, as in rising, as in bungalows on stilts, as in stork, as in _____ standing one-legged in the sea, as in wave, as in under. 4. *Feet.* As in bare, as in brown, as in crimson toes, as in flip flops, as in no snow boots, bread-bags, crumb-stuck socks. 5. *Free.* As in purple sparkle banana seat bike, as in gift from _____, as in light 'til 9 p.m., as in grownups shitfaced on sangria, as in making out with Matt Matera, as in first French kiss, as in night sky Milky Way chalky smear, as in light pollution, as in. 6. *Sun.* As in star, as in baby oil, as in slathered, as in crisscrossed tan lines, as in solar system, as in Andromeda, as in universe. 7. *Light.* As in sunrise, as in tiptoe outside, as in toenails shimmering with dew, as in being put to bed while it's still. 8. *Station Wagon.* As in yellow, as in way way back, as in emissions, as in climate change, as in lost mile of beach, as in disappeared. 9. *Refugee.* As in stranded, as in sinking, as in rooftop, as in sleep away camp over, as in can't go home, as in no home. 10. *Done.* As in Earth turning on its axis, as in Earth orbiting its star, as in bright face of Americas spun away from the sun, as in lightless, as in warmth seeping away, as in frozen ground, as in ice, as in _____ returning, as in January.

Once, In the Middle of the Night

Our backs are to their bedroom wall: brother, sister, me. To my left, a Super-8 camera is propped on the neighbor's shoulder. I pull my nightgown tight over my knees. The sheets on the bed are yellow roses. The doctor has a ponytail and high-fives my stepfather. He announces, *There's the head!* My little sister keeps trying to climb up on the bed and I hold her back, force her closer into my armpit.

At the screening, there is wine, hummus. Olive oil and paprika pool on the creamy surface. We sit on the couch: brother, sister, me. Mother hands me the swaddled baby, who lies like a lozenge in my lap. The projector whirs. There we were, filing in, sliding down the wall. Just audible between her wails, the sweet airy sound of breath being sucked in and out, through a toothless space. My brother, teaching himself to whistle.

Camp, 1979

She sits on the splintered wooden steps, alone. The smell of wet canvas
Mixes with a breeze off the lake. Behind her, six cots,

Striped mattresses cottony and thick. She lays out her plaid sleeping bag,
Dislodges a scab and brings it to her mouth, watches them retreat:

Mother, stepfather, stray younger siblings. Her little sister's hair
Flies up and a tiny butterfly barrette drops to the dirt. Flat on her back

On the slatted platform, she stares at the cobwebs lacing the peaked frame,
The seeping beads of dew, dark speckles of mold. A daddy longlegs

Walks across her thighs. She considers pinching him up by one leg
And chucking him out the back as she will hundreds of times that month

At the request of squealing tent-mates. Soon the lunch gong will ring and
She will stand, grind the barrette into the ground with her heel, take

Her seat in the dining hall, wake at midnight for a starry swim.
She lets him move along.

1980s

My thirteenth summer Danny scored tickets to the midnight
Rocky Horror Picture Show and a baggie

Of Black Beauties on the same day. We went out my bedroom window,
Down the tree and past the cemetery which spooked us

Like the time we were little and poked through the attic with flashlights
To run our fingers along the smooth metal of my uncle's

Old machete. We sank down in our seats and Danny pulled capsules
apart—we inhaled white powder. Rolls of toilet paper sailed overhead.

Accident

It happened at least once a year, the ER doors
Slid open. Her lip her chin her knee her palm,
Here comes another one. The nurse's sigh
Was gentle.

The ER doors slid open. Bloodied towel
A child's testament. Nurse's voice
A hushed penumbra, doctor's lamp seared
Apple flesh, cleaved wide.

A girl, a bloodied towel. Her mother
Said, *I had no idea.* Sun-bright, the silver needle
Stitched ragged flesh, split open. Mother
Said, *sorry, sorry.*

Mother wept, *I didn't believe her.* The girl drifted
On narcotic waves. Mother
On the phone, sorry, sorry. *You know, you know,
She's accident prone.*

The girl dreamed white-hot needles, floated navy narcotic
Oceans. Mother, insistent, *I had no idea.*
A girl, a prophecy. *Accident prone.* It happened
At least once a year.

Natural History

Being courted along with my mother, resting a cheek
On the raised wool of his suit jacket where shoulder meets arm.

It is in the thunder and the lightning
It is in the branches of the trees

Running my thumb along the stiffened seam, chipped blue whale
Sways from the ceiling. He swings me onto his shoulders, says, It's not real.

It is in the waves and the starfish's severed limb
It is in the silver undersides of the leaves

She irons a navy pocket flat, smell of rusted steam
Fills the room. She says, I married him because he was good with you.

It is in the sandstorm in the Sahara
It is in the sculpting of the dunes

Remember how you'd swing between us? I fold her question
Into my backpack, kick past her through the screen's ragged flap.

It is in the throats of the birds
It is calling, Erica, Erica, Erica, Erica, Erica

Yellow House

She said, Come visit me sometime
in my little house in the woods.
We wound our bikes through the forest
behind the baseball fields,

Danny chalked marks on trees and
I chanted—boulder, right, split-trunk maple,
left. It was the tiniest house!
It sat at the end of a narrow path choked

with roots that caught my front wheel
until I had to hop off and walk. I hovered
by the door
with my dusty summer feet,

Danny reclined on the couch.
She said, How old are you two?
Danny inverted his concave chest. I'm 12.
she's 11.

The rug smelled of spores
and darkness. She brought out a little pipe
cut from stone and leaned down
to hold it to my mouth. Her enormous breasts

had a life of their own, climbing up under
her chin and resting there.
She flicked the lighter and said,
just inhale

gently. A plate of chocolate chip cookies appeared
and then the cookies were crumbs.
We went back and back
until the woods became our own

and clouds took up residence
behind our eyes.
I biked one last time
to that house where smoke and incense

yellowed the curtains. Danny's clothes
were stacked in a neat pile
on the bedroom floor.
I fell asleep and dreamed no dreams. Weeks later

Danny said, We tripped that day. I shrugged.
I had moved on
to daytime boys who knocked me off my bike
and pinned me to the ground,

to nighttime boys whose tongues and hands
and hushed cracked voices sparked
a sublime hunger, insatiable—
better.

The Winter Inside

Echoes the winter outside. Every day has me pawing
Through leaden wool while door after wardrobe door latches

Behind. This Narnia longer than growing out bangs
When I was twelve and my sister turned a perfect pirouette,

Hair tucked in a bun. Her fingers smoothed
My fraying braid after I slipped on the ice walking home,

Grabbed the neighbor's aluminum fence, razored
My hands to shreds. Spilled fruit punch,

Ate sweetened snow, blood-salted. Permitted
That first winter's entry.

Loops

    Timmy Hatch's drunk mother's Subaru shimmies and skids
around snow-filled, speed-bumped parking lot, slides
horizontal across black ice. Timmy swigs Schnapps I pull

    from the red and yellow CB jacket I bought second hand
for fifty bucks, a fortune in cash from babysitting for Judge Gray
and his jazzercised wife in their riverside mansion where, stoned,

    I put the kids—Atticus, Clement, Beckett and Elizabeth—to bed
up the back stairs, which I thought *were* the stairs until I wandered
through the swinging kitchen door into a vast, snowy living room:

    white couches, high pile shag that held my footprints like sand,
floor-to-ceiling windows and beyond, the ice-edged river.
The veined marble mantle held beachy posed photos—

    billowing linen shirts, sun-bleached tow-heads, Elizabeth's mane
in hundreds of braids fastened with orthodontic elastic bands,
beads weighing down her pretty head. Timmy says, *Spin!*

    Pretend you're on the highway. Pretend I'm not here. Jerks
the wheel, brakes squeal. We slide sideways into the soft side
of a snow bank. Timmy's hand grips my skull, closes.

    Maybe Mexico, Cabo, sieved-sugar sand, a girl twining tiny
braids into my hair, braids that click out a percussive song
as I spin angels across the sand. Timmy yells, *Not the fucking brake!*

And What Was It Like
    for C.

To have been loved? To have alighted new each waking day
On the glassy surface of your own untouched mind,

To have taken a breath and a brush and begun—
Sprawled on the pink and orange hooked rug you made

Together, one at each end hook hook hooking
Until you met in the middle? And when she made you almond tea

In her mother's thin blue Limoges, cups and saucers
Brought from Wales in straw-packed crates

Through Ellis Island with its eye-hooks and lice checks,
And set it silently beside your scribbling hand

So as not to disturb the artist—
You. What was it like?

Was it like standing in a crowd on the edge of New York Harbor,
Sipping juice through a peppermint stick stuck in a lemon half,

Seeing past the knotted riggings of tall ships
To Lady Liberty's torch raised against a sky dripping with fireworks

And knowing she lit up just for you?

Lucifer

When the cool blue light emitted from the hidden star
Had traveled more than thirty years through galaxies frozen,
Galaxies flaming,

Had bent around planets lush with azure seas,
Planets with saloons lining
Sunken streets,

Had illuminated the powdery mountains and lava-banked rivers
Of that night he kneeled
At the bed,

Its wintry glare threatened to split me
Into twin moons, cast into
Infinite orbit.

It came in through the eyes
Glittering and flashing,
Ten thousand lionfish breaking the mirrored surface.

The Girl in the Bed

wants a witness, other than that girl in the doorway, lounging, rolling a Tootsie pop around in her mouth, looking through the bed-girl to the pop-up camper in the backyard, wings spread as if for liftoff, exhaling its winter must. A witness to last summer, to her body crammed into the mildewed apex of the wing-bed, the mathematical squares of screen imprinted on her cheek, the hand that moved deliberately across the flannel sleeping bag unzipped to lie flat. A witness other than that doorway girl rolling her eyes, clicking her lollipop, who rose from the bed-girl's body and hovered on the aluminum ceiling, refusing to throw even a glance at the figure lying stock-still on the thin mattress, as if she were textile, furry, made for touching.

1980s

By tenth grade the boys drank instead of smoked so I accessorized
With a sterling flask lifted from my father's desk. The basketball player

From up Liberty Street would throw pebbles at my bedroom window and
Pin me among the crumbs under the dining room table. Prom night,

In the sunken seat of the limo he raised the palmed flask to my mouth
And poured until I pushed him away.

Leap
      based on a family photo circa 1970

A cement wall. The girl's feet just off the edge. Midair, she touches nothing. His outstretched arms, her body. Black bangs straight across her forehead, his Roman nose in profile, his smiling mouth. Mittens dangle from a red string that gets tangled when she, with great concentration, spreads her coat on the floor, slips her arms in and flips it over her head. He wears black leather gloves. Do his hands still hold a trace of their smell, when, in the middle of the night, he covers her eyes? That sky. Bleak, yes. Branches claw, scrape. Form a hazy lattice ladder she can't see.

Breezy Point, Queens

     Jagged carapaces razor our feet. Tens of thousands of shells,
mass grave of bivalves churned, cracked open, spat out
wet and useless on their way to sand,
to powder.
     A mile from bungalow to surf, my brother gauges this trek
daily, red pedometer dragging down
the exhausted waistband of his polyester, star-spangled suit,
baring an avian hip-bone
a few years still from the adolescent male rip
of abdominals, low-slung Lees.
How small the body
of an eight-year-old boy.
     Uncle Bill, of the fascinating two bellybuttons—
appendix, our mother said, but I believed he'd somehow been attached to
two mothers—tiptoes among the remains
in faded white slip-ons,
girls' shoes, I thought and had refused to wear mine.
     Fly like me! I call, and run ahead, soles, skin, cells, nerve endings
impervious
to hot sand, then belt out
You're The One That I Want, oo-oo-oo,
so far ahead by then, alone
with the sizzle
when my feet hit the water,
the metallic taste of blood when I bite my lip,
the thousand-needled tingle of saltwater in my nose.
     If there is pain and if
it is mine, by the time the clamoring family
unties their shoes,
         I'll be sitting cross-legged on the ocean floor, willing my lungs
         to cooperate
         long enough to beat
                 my brother's record.

Were This the House

Where my parallel self slept,
where I'd sketch in three older brothers
to stand watch like German Shepherds—
she and I would face each other

cross-legged on the plush rug,
she holding the soiled yarn taut,
ponytail winding its end into her mouth,
me threading my fingers

through crisscrossed lattice,
our foreheads touching in concentration,
pyramid of stacked jacks waiting
for her to fly

through onesies, twosies,
her silver bracelets scraping the wood
in metronomic time—
were this that twinned world,

were I ever able to meet that girl
whose shiny mane swishes in my dreams,
the sun would throw back its face and laugh.
A plate of cookies would appear at our feet.

Erica Bodwell was born in Ann Arbor, Michigan to an Israeli father and an American mother. She has lived in Concord, New Hampshire for the past 25 years where she practices corporate law, write poems and climbs mountains. Her poems have appeared in *PANK, Crab Fat, Minerva Rising, White Stag, APIARY, The Fem, Coal Hill Review, HeART, Barnstorm, Hot Metal Bridge, The Tishman Review* and other journals. This is her first chapbook.

www.ingramcontent.com/pod-product-compliance
Lightning Source LLC
LaVergne TN
LVHW041521070426
835507LV00012B/1721